...berto Donati

THE DOLOMITES

The Dolomites of Sesto Ampezzo Gardena and Fassa

Catinaccio Pale of San Martino Dolomites of Brenta

Esclusivista di vendita
VALER
Via Tomaso Gar - Tel. 981784
TRENTO

Edito e stampato dalla

Narni - Terni 1985

THE DOLOMITES

Perhaps no other region in the Alpine chain has given rise to so much interest as the Dolomites, and for such different reasons. Mountaineers, geologists, poets and naturalists have all explored, studied and admired this quite unique and marvellous world. In recent years, with the coming of mass-tourism, winter sports and the return to nature, the Dolomites dominate the attention of a vast and ever-increasing public. The Alps boast much higher and more eminent peaks, gigantic massifs lying steep and irregular in the mantle of the immense glaciers. And yet, those who have contemplated the triad of Cime di Lavaredo or the legendary Catinaccio, or those who have marvelled at the bold architecture of the Dolomites of Brenta, Pale di San Martino and Sassolungo, are acquainted with the mysterious charm of these mountains. Those poetical legends born out of the imagination of the shepherds and mountainfolk of ancient times, spring to the mind: you can almost discern the fabulous castles of Fanes in the bizarre and elegant structures of the rocks, and every evening in the splendour of the sunset, the enchanted roses of King Laurino bloom on the gray faces of Catinaccio; in the moonlit nights you can picture the tiny dwarfs spinning the rays of moonlight to clothe the beautiful Dolomite summits, which for this reason are named the « Pallid Mountains ».

The real history of the Dolomites, named after the Frenchman Deodat de Dolomieu who was the first person to study its geological aspects, is written in the actual structure of the mountains. The seams of porphyry flows and tufaceous beds are identified by the scientist as being the magma of the enormous eruptions that convulsed the region in remote times. The clear traces of coral and the abundant fossils embedded in the rocks are proof of just how these mountains might have originated from the coral colonies and the sedimentation of the limestone remains of micro-organisms which thrived in teeming numbers in the sea of Tetide, the then primitive Mediterranean. It was this combination together with the overlapping of entirely different phenomena that helped to determine the rich landscape of the Dolomites: the compact coral reefs and banks of volcanic origin have been transformed by the incessant action of the intense cold, rain and wind into steep, multiform mountains and fertile land covered with pastures and dense forests. Even the appearance, which is typical of the dolomitic group, with its predominant sharp vertical and horizontal contours, is a consequence of the very nature of these rocks: the Dolomites were subjected to the titanic forces which raised and corrugated the Alpine chain and were, in turn, broken into massive blocks furrowed with ridges and fissures which the wind has sculptured into towers, steeples and slender spires.

Mountaineering in the Dolomites began with a notable delay, with respect to the western Alps, more than seventy years after the conquest of Monte Bianco: nevertheless, its story has always been reserved a chapter on its own, due to the characteristics of the reliefs and rocks of the Dolomites and also the climbing techniques which they call for. Mount Pelmo was conquered in 1857 by the Englishman John Ball, while in the following decade, the Viennese Paul Grohmann began a systematic exploration of the region, going through valleys and passes and conquering, one by one, all the principal peaks, from Tofane to Marmolada, from Cristallo to Cima Grande di Lavaredo. After this exploratory phase, it is the turn of the minor, but more difficult peaks, and so the search began on those peaks which had already been reached for faster and more demanding routes. It was an era packed with fantastic ventures and famous names like Paul Preuss and Hans Dulfer, which culminated with the daring 6 degree feats of Emil Solleder on Furchetta and on Civetta in 1925, and then those of Emilio Comici, of the Dimai brothers, and of Ettore Castiglioni. In these more recent years, which are characterised by the increasing use of artificial means, man has overcome the impossible as demonstrated by the extremely direct routes and « the course of the falling teardrop » which have been traced on the most dizzy precipices.

If the Dolomites are so famous today, the merit should be awarded to the mountaineers who were the first to discover how much light and beauty reign in this corner of the earth. The old villages have become international tourist centres and relaxing holiday resorts; but tourism has not suffocated the cultural values and ancient traditions which are even more alive today in the artistic handicrafts, in the picturesque costumes and the harmonious sound of the Ladin tongue. In spite of the very thick network of roads which stretches across the length and breadth of the region, the world of motorisation and cement has carefully respected the nature and landscape: the Dolomites boast some of the most interesting natural parks in the Alps. In the space of a few decades, the number of mechanical lifts has multiplied and today, you can go up to Tofane and Marmolada by cable-car; but still the pallid Dolomite summits preserve intact their primeval charm. Every summer, these pleasant valleys are filled with crowds of holidaymakers and tourists all in search of some sun, meadows and forests and some pure, fresh air. And in winter, the bright snow-covered slopes are enlivened by the cheerful evolutions of skiers: it was not by mere chance that the Dolomites hosted the Olympic Winter Sports in 1956 and the World Skier's Championship in 1970. The actual and more vivid appearance of the Dolomites is born out of this interlacing of themes and impressions, this variety of experiences and sensations which greets the visitor framed by woods, open fields and mountains.

Dai tipi della Litografia Artistica Cartografica - Firenze

THE DOLOMITES of SESTO

Our itinerary in the realm of the « Pallid Mountains » begins with the charming valley of Sesto, which is the southernmost among the Dolomite valleys. This first encounter with the multiform and fairytale world of the Dolomites will straightaway reveal itself to be of great interest, because among the mountainous groups which form the Dolomites of Sesto stand out some of the noblest and steepest architecture in the region: for the moment it is enough to mention Tre Cime di Lavaredo and the superb Croda dei Toni. The north-eastern boundary of this complex is marked by the short stretch of Val Pusteria lying between Dobbiaco and San Candido, then by the valley of Sesto and the upper valley of Comelico, separated by the easy pass of Monte Croce. In this area the landscape is extremely varied and fascinating: the valleys which we mentioned earlier are generally very wide, covered with green meadows and woods, and it is this radiant beauty which renders the unadorned faces of the Dolomites even more majestic outstretched towards the blue heavens above. Here, above San Candido, we have the jagged crest of Rocca dei Baranci, beyond which on entering the valley of Sesto we see opening up before us the magnificent valley of Campodidentro wedged between the groups of Rondoi-Baranci and Tre Scarperi. The beautiful face of Cima di Sesto – see plate on the right – rising up above the dark firs, dominates the valley of Sesto; straight after the town you meet the crossroads leading to the romantic Val Fiscalina which penetrates deep into the heart of the dolomitic complex towards the imposing Croda dei Toni. Ascending to the pass of Monte Croce, where the Front lines ran during the First World War, the eye beholds a long series of peaks and, standing out among these like the ramparts of a Cyclopian castle, are the superb Croda Rossa, Cima Undici and Monte Popera. With the descent into verdant Comelico, other spectacular views come into sight of the rocky spur, cut open by hollows and ravines, which extends from Cima Bagni to Monte Aiarnola, dominating Auronzo.

The southern slopes of the Dolomites of Sesto, though of a different character, are nevertheless just as suggestive, delimited by Val d'Ansiei, Val Manzon and by the carirage-way which leads from Misurina up to the Auronzo shelter near the pass of Longeres. Here, the dolomitic world unveils itself in all its natural beauty with the steep massif of Cima Dodici, or Croda dei Toni, and the smooth dizzy faces of Tre Cime di Lavaredo. The narrow valley of Landro, washed by the river Rienza, individuates the western boundary of this dolomitic complex, offering fabulous panoramic slits of Cime di Lavaredo, Cima Bulla and Croda dei Baranci.

The abovementioned itinerary takes in various towns that are often frequented as holiday resorts, and can be followed almost entirely on trafficable roads, thus rendering these mountains particularly accessible from whichever direction you choose. In spite of the modest expanse of the Dolomites of Sesto, there are numerous shelters linked by a thick network of trails which offer the possibility of making a series of crossings and excursions of rather uncommon interest. Therefore, all that remains for us to do is to draw nearer to these awe-inspiring Dolomites and discover, one by one, all the groups and peaks which they comprise.

The Róndoi-Baranci Group

The north-western extreme of the Dolomites of Sesto constitutes the Róndoi-Baranci group, which is distinctly delimited by the valleys of Campodidentro and Rimbon and the deep valley of Landro. Towards Pusteria, in the North, the terrain descends in a gentle slope covered with woods: hidden away among these woods are the sources of the Drava, while on the opposite slope rises the Rienza, a tributary of the Isarco, so that the Róndoi-Baranci mountains lie on the dividing line between the Danube and Adige basins. The group is articulated in three short chains divided by the Lago and Baranci passes. The southern part, etched with bare valleys and barren gravel hollows, consists of the ridge comprising the two Bulla peaks and culminating with Croda dei Róndoi, 2,873 m.; in the centre of the photograph below, taken from the Lavaredo pass, standing out from the others is the square East face of Croda Rondoi – the name is derived from the dialectal term used to indicate the swifts which live in these crags. In the northern sector, Croda dei Baranci and the high crest of Rocca dei Baranci, 2,966 m., rise up above the others dominating San Candido with a spectacular succession of spires and towers.

The story of mountaineering in the Rondoi-Baranci group begins in the epoca of the pioneers and some of the first ascents bear such great names as Grohmann and Michael Innerkofler; still the value of this group has not been fully evaluated, perhaps on account of the nearby Tre Cime di Lavaredo which enchant all the mountaineers.

The Tre Scarperi shelter, starting point of the excursions in the Róndoi-Baranci group, can be reached either by car or by taking a delightful walk through the woods in the Campodidentro valley. Here is a bright scene of buttercups in full bloom in the Campodidentro valley, and in the background there is Cima di Sesto and Punta dei Tre Scarperi.

The Tre Scarperi Group

From the Tre Scarperi shelter you can also make the extremely interesting, though by no means easy excursion of the group of the same name, crossing over the Lavina Bianca pass and then descending into Val Fiscalina. This itinerary will take you right into the heart of the group within sight of the titanic Punta dei Tre Scarperi; equally suggestive is the scenery offered by this regal summit and by the other subordinating peaks to those who view it from upper Val Fiscalina – see plate below – or from the Campodidentro valley, which mark the boundary of the group. The southern limit takes in Val Sassovecchio, the Toblin pass and the Grande dei Rondoi pass, which was crossed by the line of fire during the Great War, and where today the remains of military emplacements can still be seen.

In the North, the tall steep Cima di Sesto crowns the principal chain of Tre Scarperi, while on the southern slope a bare, undulating plateau stretches out on which, isolated from the rest, rise Torre dei Scarperi, Sasso di Sesto and Torre Toblin. The majestic rocky crest, arranged like an amphitheatre around the morainic deposits of Lavina Bianca, represents the major attraction of the group. Here, following one another separated only by very high passes, are the flat and massive Lastron dei Scarperi, the sharp peaks of Lavina Bianca, Piccola dei Scarperi and Punta dei Tre Scarperi, which in all its 3,145 metres constitutes the major relief of the Dolomites of Sesto. The highest summit was also the most attractive to mountaineers of the last century and, therefore, it was the first of the mountains of Sesto to be conquered, in July 1869, by Paul Grohmann and by the guide Peter Salcher and Franz Innerkofler, the same persons who only a month later were to climb Cima Grande di Lavaredo.

The dolomitic massif of Tre Scarperi dominates the trail leading to the shelter of the same name, like a mythical sailing-ship in a sea turned to stone.

Fields, forests and mountains all go to make up the simple, never-ending beauty of the Alpine landscape; here is a bright view of Val Fiscalina during haytime, and in the background rises Croda dei Toni.

The Group of Popera

The eastern sector of the Dolomites of Sesto is occupied entirely by the steep chain which runs from Croda Rossa of Sesto to Cima Bagni, and then peters out spreading towards Val d'Auronzo in Mount Aiarnola. In the centre of the group dominates the barrier of Cima Undici – 3,092 m. – cut by deep gullies which accentuate the impetus of the crest, all scalloped in a crescendo of spires and pinnacles; then, almost without warning, the profile of this architecture widens and stretches out: the mountain appears to calm down with the rounded peaks of Cresta Zsigmondy and Monte Popera, formed out of the huge horizontal dolomitic slabs. This is a view of the group of Popera as seen from the Zsigmondy-Comici shelter – see plate below – placed at the head of upper Val Fiscalina. Perhaps the eastern slope is even grander: the massive chain which unites Croda Rossa, Cima Undici and Monte Popera bends itself around the silent Popera valley forming a rocky amphitheatre with its very high walls.

This is the group of eastern Dolomites in which the largest number of routes have been traced. The first ascent was carried out in 1878 by Michael Innerkofler, who reached Cima Undici by climbing the south-west face. Today, at a distance of nearly 100 years, the group of Popera offers both to the mountaineer as well as the excursionist, extremely ample possibilities, thanks to the construction of new shelters, bivouacs high up in the mountains, footpaths and well-equipped mountaineering routes; we recall the « Strada degli Alpini » (the mountaineers' road), a long but exciting itinerary which starts from the Zsigmondy-Comici shelter, crosses over the western face of Cima Undici at an altitude of 2,500 m., then passes over the Sentinella pass and down to the Antonio Berti shelter in the Popera valley.

Behind the rocky rib in the vicinity of the plateau lakes, emerge the peaks of Cima Undici and Croda dei Toni.

Sunrise behind Torre Undici, a sharp tooth which juts out from the side of Cima Undici.

Croda dei Toni

Here we are at the foot of the queen of the Dolomites of Sesto, the magnificent « Croda dei Tuoni » (crags of thunderbolts), which uncontested, dominates Val Fiscalina and Val d'Ansiei on the opposite side. Croda dei Toni, rising solitary and imposing, is formed of a gigantic bastion of Dolomia Principale which stands out sheer against the sky. The massive pyramid of the North face — see plate on the right, with the Zsigmondy-Comici shelter — springs up from the gravel, which the age old demolition work of the rain and ice has accumulated at its feet, by an amazing height of 800 metres. On one side it is crowned by the agile peaks of Cima Piccola, Dame Vicentìne and Piccolissima, while on the other side it is flanked by the smooth face of Anticima. Following the trail which leads to the Giosuè Carducci shelter in the upper Giralba valley, after having crossed the Giralba pass, unexpectedly before us stands the superb Croda dei Toni stretching southwards, with its numerous peaks all leaning one against the other to form an enormous wall.

To the mountaineer, the group of Croda dei Toni, referred to also as Cima Dodici, constitutes a field of action of great interest, with numerous, very demanding routes. The two guides of Pusteria, Michael and Johann Innerkofler, were the first to conquer the peak of Croda dei Toni — 3,094 m. — in 1875, climbing up via the frozen gully which streaks across the West face.

Finally, a brief mention of the mountainous cluster of Cima Una, situated North of Croda dei Toni but which does not belong to this group; the photograph below illustrates the imposing pillar of Cima Una, on the left, and the jagged crest of Crode Fiscaline as viewed from the valley of Sassovecchio.

The Paterno Group

Between the undulating, barren plateaux of Pian di Cengia and Alpe dei Piani, on which there are three resplendent blue lakes, rises up the isolated powerful mass of dolomitic rocks which go to form the principal cluster of the Paterno Group. Superb and colossal they dominate the whole horizon: Tre Scarperi in the North, Cima Dodici in the East, and on the opposite side the imposing and grand Tre Cime di Lavaredo. Even though the peaks of the Paterno group are of a modest height, especially when compared to these giants, they enjoy deserved fame among the mountains of the Dolomites of Sesto, for the varied architecture of the entire complex and the tortured sculptural forms of the singular peaks. This short and jagged chain, cut by various passes, bends between the bastion of Croda Passaporto and the beautiful pyramid of mount Paterno, to be precise: on this page we have a glimpse of Croda Passaporto from the Lavaredo pass, which separates the Paterno group from Tre Cime.

The first mountaineer to reach the summit of Paterno – 2,746 m. – was Künigl, in 1882; in the following years all the peaks of the group were conquered, one by one, and new routes were opened, some of which represented truly exceptional feats. Today the Paterno group is one of the favourite destinations of Alpine tourism in the mountains of Sesto, due to the easy accessibility, the numerous shelters and, most of all, the beauty of the panorama which is viewed from here. A tour of the group is highly suggestive, taking in the shelters of Locatelli, Pian di Cengia and Lavaredo, situated right at the feet of the summits bearing the same names.

Near the Toblin pass, which opens out between the Paterno group and that of Tre Scarperi, stands the Antonio Locatelli shelter – at 2,438 m. – in a magnificent panoramic position right in front of Tre Cime. This vantage point in the heart of the Dolomites of Sesto, makes the Locatelli shelter the ideal starting point for the crossings and climbs in the groups of Tre Scarperi and Paterno – see photograph above – and Tre Cime di Lavaredo.

Tre Cime di Lavaredo

Perhaps in no other part of the Dolomites as in front of the Tre Cime di Lavaredo have we been stirred so deeply by the beauty of these mountains; the majesty of its volume, the harmony of its forms and colours, the purity of its architectural structure, noble and elegant like a cathedral, all contribute towards making this fantastic triad the highest expression in the dolomitic region. This compact and magnificently isolated group comprises three principal peaks which represent the residue of an ancient bastion, eroded and fragmented (or should we say sculptured because the result is truly wonderful) by rain, wind and ice. The slender Cima Piccola, 2,853 m., Cima Grande, 2,999 m., in the centre and Ovest, 2,973 m., follow one another in regular alignment, tied together in an harmonious embrace. From the same foundations as Cima Piccola, rise up Punta di Frida and Piccolissima, which are lower but equally elegant. In the plate on the left they can be seen together with the famous Spigolo Giallo.

The entire story of dolomitic mountaineering is written on the faces of Tre Cime, from the first daring pioneers to the more recent enterprises, animated by a quest for both new and more difficult routes. In 1869, Paul Grohmann conquered Cima Grande with the guides Salcher and Innerkofler, climbing up the South face; later Michael Innerkofler opened the « common » routes to Cima Ovest and Piccola; in 1933, Emilio Comici of Trieste affronted the fearsome Spigolo Giallo and traced, together with G. Dimai, the first route on the North face of mount Grande, which until then was considered unconquerable. Finally, among the new routes opened by modern climbers on the sheer northern faces, we can mention Via dei Sassoni. a perfect vertical line running down the middle of the North face of Cima Grande, traced by the mountaineers Siegert, Uhner and Kauschke, in seventeen days of climbing in freezing winter temperatures.

The tour of Tre Cime di Lavaredo is an easy excursion and, at the same time, of exceptional interest because it allows you to enjoy an infinite number of views of the three fantastic summits in a progressive and varied play of perspective, light and shadows. From the Auronzo shelter, linked with Misurina by a wide road, you can reach the Locatelli shelter by crossing the Col di Mezzo pass, and then from there you carry on towards the Lavaredo shelter. From the Lavaredo pass you can get a glimpse of the three lofty sisters (in the foreground is Piccolissima): even more impressive if you think that a man has managed to climb up those bare walls. Returning to the starting point, facing South, the eye meets a forest turned to stone, bristly with spires, pointed pinnacles, sharp towers and crests: this is the group of Cadini di Misurina, as shown in the photograph below.

Lake

The most famous of all is the view of the southern faces of Tre Cime di Lavaredo, with the regular stripes of the ridges forming a grand flight of steps: here is a suggestive glimpse during winter as well as a view at the beginning of summer, when the mountains are still covered with snow while the shores of the lake are cheered up by a wonderful array of buttercups in bloom. The oposite side is dominated by the solemn amphitheatre formed by the northern walls of Sorapiss.

Misurina

The beautiful lake Misurina is set like a precious emerald among the mountains of Tre Cime di Lavaredo, the Cadini group and the Dolomites of Ampezzo. It is the most important natural lake of Cadore. Misurina, easily accessible from Cortina d'Ampezzo via the Tre Croci pass, is a very popular holiday resort and also the destination of many pleasant walks to view the picturesque scenery offered by these superb mountains which encircle the tiny, blue mirror of water.

THE DOLOMITES OF AMPEZZO

Cortina d'Ampezzo: one of the most renowned spots among the holiday resorts and winter sports stations of the entire Alpine range. It certainly owes its fame to the magnificent ski-runs, the numerous modern ski-lifts and cable-ways and, also, to the Olympic Ice-rink Stadium, inherited from the 1956 Winter Olympics; its bustling streets fervent with life, and the elegant shops, the thousands of sporting and social events, all no doubt create a big attraction. However, the true wealth of Cortina, long before the man-made creations, lies in nature's own inestimable gift: the dazzling beauty of its wide, bright valleys, the green meadows and thick forests of fir-trees, the murmuring brooks and, most of all, the silent and firm embrace of its mountains.

The Dolomites of Ampezzo are those mountainous groups which overlook the pleasant valley of Cortina forming the inimitable crown which extends across almost the whole horizon: on the southern slope, facing the sun, the arc of these mountains is broken at the point where the « Gateway of the Dolomites » opens onto verdant Cadore, watched over by the noble peaks of Pelmo and Antelao. From whichever angle you choose to admire these mountains, be it from a road, a footpath at the bottom of a valley, or from a flower-covered meadow, the view which you get is truly suggestive. Nowhere else are these Dolomites so awe-inspring, standing steep and powerful and displaying all their fanciful charm in the agile crags hanging suspended between the blue sky and the green pastures below. Here we have the majestic group of Sorapiss which stretches forward with the undulating snow-covered slopes of Alpe Faloria; rising up in front of this, on the other side of the Tre Croci pass, is Cristallo scintillating with ice and snow, which in ancient times was known as « Croda de Bartoldo »: in fact, one of the most poetical legends of the Dolomites relates how there was a princess whose castle stood on these very mountains, and who married a very humble shepherd called Bertoldo. On the opposite side stands the grand, three-peaked massif of Tofane, while in the North, the Ampezzo basin is closed in by the picturesque and solitary Alpe di Senes crowned by Croda del Becco and the blood-red Croda Rossa. Finally, the turreted wall of Croda del Lago stands facing South, flanked by the Nuvolau group with the very unique Cinque Torri. These mountains have witnessed the very first mountaineering expeditions in the Dolomites, dating back to more than a century ago, and which have already become legends. In 1857, the Englishman John Ball climbed up to the peak of Monte Pelmo, considered the « throne of the Eternal Father ». Only a few years later, the then very young Paul Grohmann, founder of the Austrian Mountaineering Club, arrived in the Dolomites to show mountaineers the magic of the unexplored kingdom of the « Pallid Mountains »; the merit should go to him for having created the first guides of the Ampezzo region, who, incidentally, were chosen from the most skilled chamois hunters, namely Lacedelli, Dimai, Siorpaes. This tradition is still carried on today by the expert guides and the fantastic « Squirrels » of Cortina. These mountains have another tale to tell to those who climb up the numerous footpaths and over the rock-piton ladder routes across gravel hollows and passes and clambering over ledges and rocky faces up to the summits: it is the story of the long war years, 1915-17, which have left their scars in the trenches, caverns and tunnels dug out of the rocks, the military stations and fallen-down huts.

Recently, an interesting enterprise was carried out to restore the old military trails in the area lying between Alpi di Fanes and the group of Tofane, and others are still in the process of being prepared. These same paths, which at one time divided men, have today been turned into « paths of friendship ».

Even before setting foot in the Ampezzo basin, visitors who arrive in Cortina from the direction of Val Pusteria are greeted with the view of the northern faces of mount Cristallo, all faceted and resplendent like a diamond and mirrored in the delightful lake of Landro. On arrival in Misurina, here we have some more of these beautiful Ampezzo mountains which form the group of Sorapiss, revealing all its majesty in the outspread massive wall that culminates in Punta Sorapiss, 3,205 m.

Some very tough and demanding climbs on pure rock can be made in the Cristallo group, as well as some beautiful excursions and crossings, among which is the rock-piton ladder route called « Ivano Dibona » that follows a series of connecting routes dating back to the First World War. The cable-way system makes the entrance to the group from Cortina much easier, rising in two sections right up to the Staunies pass, where Guido Lorenzi's Cabin stands – 2,932 m. – the highest shelter in the Dolomites of Ampezzo. The highest peaks in this group are all concentrated in the southern sector, and the deep furrow of the Cristallo pass separates them into the distinct clusters of mount Cristallo – 3,216 m. - and Piz Popena – 3,152 m. The photographs show the Lorenzi Cabin with the North-West peak of Cristallo and Piz Popena in the back-ground; the rugged faces of Piz Popena in the foreground and Cristallo viewed from the Tre Croci pass; a view from the Ampezzo valley of the beautiful Cristallo peak in the golden sunset.

Cortina d'Ampezzo, composed mainly of large hotels and boarding houses, with its bustling streets and numerous clubs and haunts, has the typical appearance of the big tourist centres. However, if you just take a few steps out of the town centre, you can enjoy the serene beauty of the pastures and woods lying at the foot of the pale, rocky faces; here and there, you come across one of the tiny, peaceful hamlets that are scattered over the Ampezzo valley, a rustic mountain-hut, or one of the characteristic trellises on which the hay is spread out to dry. The long dolomitic cliff which forms the background of these scenes, is the chain of Pomagagnon, a projection of the Cristallo group on the mountainside of Cortina.

The Group

The western end of the green Cortina valley is closed off by a mighty wall bordered by a dark forest of fir-trees and, topping this wall, are three huge rocky domes otherwise known as the group of Tofane, which is perhaps the most famous among the Dolomites of Ampezzo.

On the Ampezzo side, where the sheer drops of Tofana di Mezzo – 3,244 m. and Tofana di Dentro – 3,237 m. – are broken by an enormous ridge of the Ra Valles plateau, there are lively ski-runs which twist and curve down the slopes, well-provided with ski-lifts and numerous shelters.

On the opposite side, the stage of many heroic battles and also, numerous outstanding mountaineering enterprises, you can view all three peaks of Tofane, streaked with ledges and gullies, and dominating the wild valley of Travenanzes. The first person to conquer all three peaks was Grohmann: since then, many great names in mountaineering have opened other beautiful routes, among which the very fast and direct « 6 degree » routes of the Squirrels of Cortina.

# of Tofane

Today, one of the most important cable-way systems in Europe, called « Freccia del Cielo » (meaning Arrow in the Sky), takes you, with three great leaps, right up to the top of Tofane di Mezzo from where the above three photographs were taken. Here, towards the South-West, we have the powerful back of Tofana di Rozes – 3,225 m. – sloping down In a series of steps, along which runs the very interesting rock-piton route of Giovanni Lipella; in the background emerges Marmolada with its famous glacier. Still from Tofana II, facing South-East, you can distinguish the very sharp Croda da Lago, Pelmo and Antelao. Finally turning towards the North, your gaze sweeps across from the dome of Tofana di Dentro to the group of Croda Rossa, then from the wide furrow of Val Pusteria right up to the Austrian Alps. The scenes from the foot of these dolomitic faces are just as suggestive: here we have the spectacular South face of Tofana di Rozes towering over the woods of Malghe Fedarola, and standing sentinel is the slender peak of Castelletto – photograph on the right – made famous by the powerful mine explosion in 1916, which gashed both flanks of the mountain.

The fantastic western faces of Tofane can be viewed from the head of the Travenanzes valley, not far from the Falzarego pass. In front of these bare, high faces, which bear the clear traces of the slow stratification process that formed these dolomitic giants, you get the charming, i n t e n s e sensation of witnessing nature at its origin. In the total silence that reigns, the only proof of the presence of man lies in the remains of the shacks and trenches of the First World War. Here, in this spot, one seems to forget that just on the other side is the valley of Cortina d'Ampezzo, bustling gaily with sporting life.

Sunrise and sunset are the two most magical moments of the day. When the mountains are still immersed in the twilight and the first rays of sunl ight up the peaks and upper crags with strokes of yellow and golden, they appear to come to life; also, when the false light of the sunset plays on the pale faces of these mountains, painting them with thousands of hues of pink, purple and burning embers.

The photographs above show, once again, the two views of Tofana di Rozes: the radiant light of sunrise gives the mountain a new aspect, highlighting in particular, the unexpected contours and size of the high South face.

And here we have two sunsets: on the left is Nuvolau, with the shelter bearing the same name, and on the right is the beautiful Croda Marcora, the southern bastion of the Sorapiss group, resplendent against the dark valley of Boite.

The towering and elegant, compact mass of mount Pelmo – 3,168 m. – rises up regal and solitary to dominate the valleys of Ampezzo and Zoldo; the summit of Pelmetto, sculptured in this same mighty Dolomite block, is similar in form and geological structure to the principal peak and separated from it by a deep incision called « Fisura » (meaning fissure).

The two photographs taken from Malga Fiorentina near the Aquileia shelter, show the western faces of Pelmo and Pelmetto, underneath which extends the small glacier of Val d'Arcia.

At the northern extreme of the Cortina valley, where the Boite has its source, the vast group of Croda Rossa of Ampezzo rises up extending from the valley of San Vigilio to the head of the Landro valley, and then it pushes on North towards the Pusteria valley. Actually, a major part of the group is formed from the limestone-dolomitic plateau of Senes and Fosses, around which rise the polychrome castle of Croda Rossa – 3,139 m. and the characteristic Croda del Becco. The latter slopes down the southern side in a flat oblique slab, while it thrusts northwards in a gigantic face that is mirrored in the delightful lake of Braies.

The entire area of the Senes Alps and the nearby Fanes Alps – the cradle of poetical legends – forms a whole natural oasis. The landscape is composed of poor, undulating pastures fed by secluded lakes or frothy waterfalls; at various points crop up gray banks of rock which were bent, broken and overturned during the epoca of the folding of the Alpine chain. Quite often, we can get a glimpse of beautiful herds of roe-deer feeding at the feet of the higher peaks.

Cinque Torri

On the other side of the Grande Strada (the main highway of the Dolomites), facing the South face of Tofana di Rozes, you will find another very impressive plateau, crowned by a jagged dolomitic ridge stretching out diagonally across the wide saddle of the Giau pass up to the Falzarego pass. Aligned along this crest are mount Gusella and Nuvolau with its shelter placed in an exceptionally panoramic position, and the mighty bastion of mount Averau – 2,648 m. – which represents the highest point of the group. The Averau plateau is a very popular resort for those wishing to make easy and enjoyable excursions, especially on account of its easy access, the numerous footpaths and shelters and also the spectacular views of the Ampezzo mountain-range, in particular, Tofane and Croda da Lago. A chair-lift will take you right up to the Scoiattoli shelter, stationed at the North-eastern extremity of this plateau, which forms a splendid balcony overlooking the Cortina valley with the sparkling mount Cristallo in the background. Here, rising up in isolated splendour, are the unique Cinque Torri of Averau (literally five towers), ancient ruins of a turreted mountain, which provides a characteristic example of the destruction of the strong dolomitic architecture. The highest and most powerful of these is Torre Grande – 2,366 m. – consisting of a gigantic, squared block of rock scarred by a deep fissure more than 150 m. high. Rising up at the latter's foot, among the sandstone and detritus, is Torre Seconda composed of three distinct pillars, Torre Latina, Torre Quarta and the oblique Torre Inglese. Even though the Cinque Torri are of a rather modest elevation, they nevertheless bear all the characteristics found in the major dolomitic faces and, therefore, constitute an ideal rock gymnasium in which to practice some short but extremely difficult acrobatic climbs.

The valley of Cortina d'Ampezzo is linked with the other dolomitic valleys by the Falzarego pass lying in the West, which is saddled by the Grande Strada of the Dolomites, in its long meanderings leading to Val d'Adige. The extreme ramification of the Nuvolau ridge and the sheer face of Piccolo Lagazuoi together with the pointed Sasso di Stria lying on the other side – forming the background to the pretty little church shown in the photograph – make the harsh and severe landscape of this important pass appear even more suggestive. A cable-car climbs with an impressive leap right to the top of Piccolo Lagazuoi – photograph above – at an altitude of 2,746 m., from which point the entire Dolomite region can be viewed.

From Falzarego you can also carry on towards Val Badia, via the Valparola pass, which is wedged between Sasso di Stria and Lagazuoi. This short itinerary gives you the opportunity of viewing, from close quarters, a severe though picturesque dolomitic group in surroundings where the silence of the Alps reigns supreme: this is the Cunturines group, also known as the Alps of Fanes, which stretches out in a majestic range of mountains convexed in the direction of Val Badia, until the lake of Limo where it rejoins the range of the Senes Alps. The principal peaks – see photograph – stand well over 3,000 metres in height, namely Piz delle Cinturines, with its wide face scarred with gorges and rocky spurs, and La Varella, which dominates the green meadows of San Cassiano.

THE DOLOMITES of GARDENA and FASSA

Lying between the Adige valley and the furrows formed by Val Badia and Cordevole is the zone of the Western Dolomites, which comprises the mountainous reliefs surrounding the valleys of Gardena and Fassa and the group of Pale di San Martino. This vast and complex area comprises diverse groups which merit much closer attention, but first of all, an outline of their general features is useful in order to point out those characteristics which are common to these superb dolomitic peaks and valleys of the region.

The squared shape of Sella stands out with its umistakable scar, formed by a wide horizontal ridge, and serves as a sure landmark. Fanning out from this important orographical cluster are the mountainous groups which crown the wide valleys listed on our itinerary. Standing out in the North are the varied geometrical forms of Pizzes da Cir and Odle, while towards the West, in front of the severe buttresses of Sella, emerges the spectacular summit of Sassolungo and Sassopiatto, which on one side dominates the Gardena Valley and the undulating grasslands of Alpe di Siusi, and on the other, the bright Canazei Valley. A long, rocky ridge stretches out from the Sassolungo massif towards the South-West and continues along the green Fassa Valley until Moena, separating it from the nearby basin of Bolzano: easily individuated along this ridge are the imposing and legendary group of Catinaccio, beautiful Roda da Vael and Latemar standing all alone and picturesque. Finally, there is Marmolada in the South, buried under the vast glacier which adds a decidedly Alpine touch to the fairy-tale world of the Dolomites.

In order to define the characteristics and appearance of these mountains, we should mention its geological structure. The so-called porphyritic platform of the upper end of the Adige river, formed from a gigantic porphyry flow of volcanic origin measuring 1,000 to 1,500 metres in thickness, constitutes one of the oldest layers in the Western Dolomites: this type of rock formation is entirely missing in the Eastern Dolomites. Another difference can be seen in the more recent layers, those dolomitic complexes formed by the coral colonies. We have in fact seen that the bare peaks of the eastern zone, namely from Tre Cime di Lavaredo to Croda dei toni and from Cristallo to Tofane, go to make up Dolomia Principale. Instead, prevailing over the valleys of Gardena and Fassa is Dolomia dello Sciliar, which has been sculptured by erosion into spires and turrets that sprout up on Catinaccio, Sassolungo and Odle: this type of Dolomia or Dolomites, which is not composed in layers, forms the framework of the Sciliar massif from which its name is derived, and the Sella group. Through the years, these mountains have managed to preserve the compact structure of their primitive cliffs with the aid of a protective film of clayey, waterproof limestone, known as « layer of Raibl », and in the case of Sella, also by a cap of Dolomia Principale.

The valleys at the foot of these peaks, together with Val Badia and the Livinallongo Valley which radiate in opposite directions towards the eastern side, all converge on the massive, isolated rocks of Sella. The bright and beautiful scenery of Gardena and Fassa, interwoven with the variegated sun-drenched grasslands, thickly wooded with fir-trees which create suggestive contrasts with the ashen and golden hues of the dolomitic faces, put these two valleys among the most renowned resorts of the Dolomites. An excellent organisation for promoting tourism works hard in exploiting this natural patrimony and these efforts are displayed in the famous holiday resorts and winter sports stations such as Ortisei, Santa Cristina and Selva di Val Gardena, Moena, Vigo and Canazei. The bright valleys which, in the past, were very industrious and populated, boast a rich cultural background which is perpetuated today in the musical cadenza of the Ladin tongue — derived from vulgar Latin — and the traditional handicraft of wood-carving.

The Odle Mountains

You can take the cable-car from Ortisei up to mount Seceda, the extreme western ramification of the Odle range, from where you will see how this group of jagged peaks, culminating in Sass Rigais which rises up in the background, seem to be aligned along the ridge separating the suggestive Funes Valley from the green grasslands of Alpe Mastlè which extend undulating towards the Gardena Valley. Even from Santa Cristina there is a thick network of paths and the cable-car of Col Raiser which will take you right to the foot of Odle, over the picturesque pastures dotted with mountain-huts, and the sparse patches of conifers on Alpe di Cisles. The name Odle – which in Ladin means « needles » – is particularly apt; in fact, from the Funes Valley these peaks appear like a dense series of sharp, pointed spires and edges, the majority of which standing decidedly upright. The two principal peaks, standing side by side, are Sass Rigais – 3,025 m. – and Furchetta of the same height; the latter is well-known among mountaineers because of its very difficult North face – plate on the right – on which Emil Solleder and Franz Weissner started, in 1925, the famous « era of the 6th degree » in the Dolomites.

Puez

The Puez plateau, lying between the groups of Odle and Sella, the Selva Valley and upper Val Badia, stretches out crowned by a series of bare dolomitic faces which, altogether, form a wild, barren labyrinth of rocks. The most beautiful and interesting peaks rise up in the southern sector, together with the massive Sassongher which dominates Covara. Here we see the tortured crest of Pizzes da Cir and the squat Col Turond, which together with the northern banks of Sella delimit the Gardena Pass, one of the four passes that open out around the Sella group. The base of Pizzes da Cir is mantled by stretches of grassland that slope down towards the Gardena Pass and during winter, these slopes are transformed into a paradise for skiers.

Rising up in front of the Corvara basin in Val Badia is an imposing turret on an irregular rocky base: it is Sassongher – 2,665 m. – lying at the South-eastern extremity of the Puez group, which is a classic dolomitic peak portraying an elegance in its contours and the mighty force of its mass.

The Gardena pass, which links the Gardena Valley with Val Badia, is viewed here from Pizzes da Cir. Looming over the thin asphalt ribbon which rises towards the pass in a close series of hairpin bends, is the Cyclopian bastion of Sella, split up into powerful buttresses among which stands out the famous Torre del Murfreid, on the right, with its characteristic rift called the « oblique death ».

The Group of Sella

A general outline of the physical features of this famous dolomitic group is very well described on the map, which illustrates its quadrilateral form with the four Ladin valleys of Badia, Gardena, Fassa and Livinallongo lying at its tips; on the sides are the very frequented passes which link these valleys and, which provide ideal starting points for excursions in this group. The Sella massif is very easy to distinguish from the other surrounding reliefs and its natural boundaries coincide with those traced by man; in fact, once across the passes of Gardena, Sella, Pordoi and Campolongo, you can tour the entire group by car following one of the most impressive itineraries in the dolomitic region.

The architecture of the Sella group is characterised, primarily, by the grandeur and compactness of the entire mass, held together by sheer rock faces and surmounted by an uneven plateau topped by some of the highest peaks. The buttresses barring the Gardena and Fassa valleys are rather square-cut and severe, cut across horizontally by the long ridge corresponding to the Raibl plateau; rising up on a mighty shelf, striped with gravel hollows, are Murfreid with its Towers and Spires, the elegant Torri di Sella and Sass Pordoi, lined like bulwarks along the wall of this Cyclopian fortress. Two deeply-set valleys descend in opposite directions from the heart of the group, namely the valleys of Mesdì and Lasties, which divide the massifs into the sub-groups of Mesules and Boè.

Here, on this page, is a glimpse of a tract of the Great Highway of the Dolomites that runs from Canazei to the Pordoi pass, framed by dark firs in the wings with the dizzy face of Piz da Clavazes rising up above; the plate on the right shows the three steep Torri di Sella towering over the grassland of the pass bearing the same name in front of Sassolungo.

The pretty Plan de Gralba basin, lying between the Sella pass and Selva di Val Gardena, is covered with fields and woods which thin out and finally cede to the bare faces of rock.

The road branches off from Plan de Gralba towards the Gardena pass and winds in a series of bends at the foot of the north-western side of Sella. This long wall, scarred with severe ravines, is called Murfreid, which means « cold wall »: looming up above the massive ridge is Torre del Murfreid, isolated from the rest – photograph below – while in the background are the Campanili del Murfreid standing side by side. The first climbers to reach this peak of Torre del Murfreid – 2,631 m. – were the Austrians Ampferer and Berger, in 1899. The plate on the right shows the zig-zag of the sheer peaks of Sass de la Leusa, which dominate both sides of the Gardena pass.

A classic excursion in the Sella group is the peak of Piz Boè. Departing from Colfosco, at the head of Val Badia, you then climb up the first tract of the valley of Mesdi, which is very barren and wild in appearance, dug out of the compact Sella mass and enclosed between two rocky walls. Rising up on one side are the steep Piz da Lec, Sasso delle Nove and Sasso delle Dieci, and soaring up on the other side are Torre Bamberger and the sharp Dent de Mesdì, considered one of the most beautiful dolomitic spires, which in this photograph stands out distinctly against the blue sky. Another itinerary, a bit more difficult this time, starts from the Gardena pass and climbs up via the rock-piton route to the Pisciadù valley, which has a very characteristic waterfall. The two trails meet in the vicinity of the Cavazza shelter, situated at the foot of Cima Pisciadù, from where you continue towards the Boè shelter – 2,871 m. – right in the heart of the Sella group. The Piz Boè peak – 3,151 m. – is easily accessible and offers a truly spectacular panorama that sweeps across the Dolomites of Ampezzo to the glaciers of Adamello and Ortles; nearby in the South, stands Marmolada imposing and majestic in its snow-white mantle of ice. During the winter season ,the Sella group offers some very enjoyable skiing excursions, with the aid of the Sass Pordoi cable-car that climbs up to almost 3,000 metres.

Sass Pordoi

When the valley and the woods higher up are already plunged in the evening shadows, the towering cliffs which are just lightly dusted with snow, live their moment of glory: it is the magical moment in which the warm glow of the sunset sets the harsh dolomitic faces aflame, making them appear golden and unreal. This view of Sass Pordoi, taken from the road leading to the Sella pass, is one of the most well-known in the Dolomites. The powerful rocky mass, with its unmistakable profile, forms the southern bastion of Sella and clearly reveals the geological composition of the group characterised by the Raibl strata that separates Dolomia dello Sciliar from the more recent Dolomia Principale.

Out of the numerous climbs made on Sass Pordoi we shall only mention the first, carried out in 1910, which bears the names of the famous guides Tita Piaz and Francesco Jori. Today, there is a quick cable-car service from the Sass Pordoi pass which, in a single run, takes you right up to the level of the Sass Pordoi summit – 2,950 m.

Another easy approach for excursions in the Sella group is provided by the narrow gravelly Lasties valley, situated on the western side, which opens onto green pastures bordered by the firs that mantle the head of the Fasso Valley in the direction of the Sella pass. This area is encircled by the imposing cliffs of Sass Pordoi and, on the other side, Piz Sella and Piz Ciavazes see photograph – which unveils to the sun its southern face interrupted halfway up by Cengia dei Camosci.

The southern wall of Sella bristles with spires and turrets and dominates the undulating grasslands, which slope down from the Pordoi pass towards the Livinallongo valley, and gather the fresh water of the Cordevole torrent. Standing out on the left is the massif of Sass Pordoi, crowned by the uppermost cable-car station.

The next plate illustrate the magnificent panorama which can be seen from the peak of Sass Pordoi. The imposing mass of Marmolada provides the main attraction, with its vast scintillating glacier, while on the horizon emerges the clear profile of the three giants of Cadore: Monte Civetta, Pelmo and Antelao.

The Group of Sassolungo

The severe, turreted mass of Sassolungo, emblem of the Gardena valley, stands dominating over the wooded hillocks that descend from the plateau of Alpe di Siusi towards Ortisei and Selva. A classic view of this group is that of the South-East side, either from the Sella pass or from Pordoi, which reveals the entire grand and elegant structure — see following plate: the scanty surface area gives particular emphasis to these mighty rocky faces, which stand over a thousand metres in height. The group of Sassolungo is illustrated on the map as a huge horseshoe with the opening in the North-West direction, and to date, it still preserves intact the structure of the primitive coral atoll. The more impressive peaks lie at the extremities of the group, while in the centre are a series of minor and rather slender peaks, among which Cinque Dita, Sasso Levante and the characteristic Dente. The western branch is constituted by the powerful ridge of Sassolungo — 3,181 m. — formed like a sugar-loaf and overlooking the Gardena Valley; the rocky mass is scarred and fragmented by numerous gullies which throw emphasis on its towers, spires and pillars. The massif of Sassopiatto — 2,964 m. — occupies the opposite side of this amphitheatre with some of its step walls looking onto the barren gravelly interior while, on the south-western flank, it is characterised by a wide, flat scarp that gently slopes down. Two small, morainic valleys run between these walls, separated by a short rocky crest, and they provide easy access to the heart of the group and to the starting points of those long, difficult routes which lead to the various summits. The story of the first ascent in the group of Sassolungo takes us back to the epoca of the pioneers of dolomitic mountaineering: in 1869, Paul Grohmann, accompanied by the famous guides Salcher and Innerkofler, conquered the highest peak.

From Santa Cristina you can go either by road or by cable-car up to Monte Pana, which is the extreme ramification of Alpe di Siusi. The high cliff of Sassolungo and Sassopiatto emerges out of this wavy green sea, shining and resplendent in the rays of the sunset. The main resting point in the group is the Vicenza shelter, situated in the midst of a magnificent amphitheatre of rock: in the photograph above, you will see the steep profile of Dente — 3,001 m. — rising up in the background.

The following plate illustrates a view of Sassolungo from the road leading to the Pordoi pass. The surging jagged summit of Punta delle Cinque Dita rises up between the two formidable walls culminating in Cima Sassolungo and the squared pyramid-shape of Sasso Levante.

Here are two more views of the morainic basins, at whose heads lie tucked away two tiny glaciers, enclosed between the enormous walls of Sassolungo and Sassopiatto and separated from them by Cima Dantersass – a Ladin word meaning «between the peaks». The photograph above shows the pointed Cinque Dita which are separated from the Sassolungo massif by the narrow saddle of the Sassolungo pass; the Toni Demetz shelter, situated on this pass in an extremely panoramic position, can be reached by cable-car from the Sella pass on the other side. The photograph below shows the sheer North-East face of Sassopiatto, with the Vicenza shelter underneath.

The massif of Sciliar, one of the most characteristic dolomitic formations, closes off the south-western side of Alpe di Siusi, and on the opposite side it dominates the wide open valley of Isarco and the Bolzano basin. The most famous section of Sciliar, formed of a flat open plateau – 2,564 m. – is linked to the Catinaccio system by the crest of Terra Rossa; on the other sides it is held up by vertical, compact walls of « Dolomia » which have been well-protected from erosion by a thin protective layer of clayey marl. Instead, in those parts where this layer has been removed, the destructing work of atmospheric agents has eroded also the dolomitic rock, so creating the isolated pointed towers of Cima Santner and Cima Euringer, which bear the names of the first mountaineers to conquer them.

The Group of Catinaccio

The long ridge uniting the groups of Sassolungo and Catinaccio spreads out from the Sella pass to the Costalunga pass and forms the right flank of the Fassa Valley, separating it from Alpe di Siusi and the Bolzano basin. Two main aspects which characterise Catinaccio, its easy access and varied features, can be verified in the actual structure of the group, which is split up into thin long chains that link up here and there giving rise to a complex system of wild glens, gravel basins and high narrow passes. The most important among these furrows is the Vajolet valley which rises in the Fassa valley and continues until the Principe pass: in its meanderings over the central part of the group, it divides the zone of Catinaccio d'Antermoia – 3,004 m. – and the picturesque Dirupi di Larsec from the narrow chain running North to South along Torri del Vajolet, Cima Catinaccio – 2,981 m. – and Roda di Vael. Catinaccio, therefore, is ideal for excursions and crossings: penetrating deep into the heart of the group you can discover, apart from the classic views such as Torri del Vajolet, some extremely unexpected features that are less well-known but not the least bit less suggestive. Its towers surging upwards, the jagged crests and, the smooth bare walls which have encountered many daring feats by famous mountaineers, all contribute to making Catinaccio very attractive to rock-climbers.

Finally, a mention should be made of the ancient legend which, during the romantic period, inspired the poetical name of Rosengarten (rosegarden). The tale narrates how at one time the faces of Catinaccio were mantled by a rose-garden inhabited by a community of dwarfs. The king of the dwarfs, called Laurino, who had kidnapped the princess Similda, was then made prisoner by the princess's brother. King Laurino finally escaped after many years, and on the way back to his kingdom he happened to glance at the beautiful roses blooming above the woods and decided, there and then, to throw a curse on them for revealing the secret of his kingdom of Dwarfs to mankind: the roses were transformed into gray rocks so that neither by day nor by night could they be seen anyone.

However, at dusk, when it is neither day nor night, the roses of King Laurino burst into bloom.

Torri del Vajolet

One of the most interesting and very popular itineraries in the Catinaccio group takes in the Vajolet valley right up until the beautiful Gardeccia basin, giving you some very picturesque sights of the jagged Dirupi di Larsec – see photograph below – and the magnificent rocky mass of Catinaccio – meaning enormous basin – is derived from this. From Gardeccia, at the boundary line between the green world of woods and meadows and the hard, severe kingdom of rock, starts the steep ascent which passes through a barren plateau where the Preuss and Vajolet shelters have been constructed, and finally, brings you to the upper basin and the Alberto I shelter, at an altitude of 2,650 m. The imposing North face of Catinaccio, Croda di Re Laurino and Torri del Vajolet dominate over the solitary and wild surroundings of the shelter which, even in the height of summer, is often covered by a light sprinkling of snow – as seen in the plate overleaf.

The short, rugged chain of Torri del Vajolet comprises six main peaks joined together in the two distinct bands of the Western and the very famous Southern « Towers ». The clear-cut contours and unrivalled steep angles have earned these peaks the reputation of having the most elegant and majestic architecture out of all the Dolomites. The « three sisters » of Vajolet, extremely popular among mountaineers, have been christened with the names of their conquerors: Torre Delago (2,790 m.), Torre Stabeler (2,805 m.), and Torre Winkler (2,800 m.), – seen from left to right in the side plate.

A very steep gorge lying between rocky walls brings us to the Vajolet and Preuss shelters — at an altitude of 2,243 m. — on the ridge that separates the Gardeccia basin from the upper valley of Vajolet; from here you can go up to the small Principe Pass shelter situated at the head of Vajolet. A footpath clambers up along the southern flank of Cantinaccio d'Antermoia, the highest tip of the group, until the pass of the same name — 2,769 — and then descends into the solitary glacial basin, which conceals the blue lake of Antermoia. Looking East from Marmolada, you can view the unusual and suggestive scene of the flat glacier and the sheer South face. The ascent to Antermoia pass — photograph below — unveils some extensive views of Torri del Vajolet and Catinaccio rising up on the other side of the deep Vajolet valley.

Latemar and Lake Carezza

The wide, grassy saddle of the Costalunga pass opens up between the extreme southern ramifications of Catinaccio and the Latemar group, which separates the upper Ega valley from the Avisio valleys. Delightful Lake Carezza is situated among the dark, thick woods which spread out at the foot of this group. The view of the jagged North face of Latemar, bristly with turrets and spires and reflected in the calm, limpid mirror formed by the tiny lake, is without a doubt one of the most famous and expressive sights in the dolomitic region. The group's features derive from the structure of the primitive coral atoll constructed on a volcanic cone: in fact, Latemar consists of a rocky crest arranged in a semi-circle around the vast detrital basin of Valsorda, giving one the impression of a desolated lunar landscape. The outer side, instead, shows the typical characteristics of the Dolomites with the steep sheer walls, scarred by deep ravines which rush headlong towards the gravel layer down below. Although the Latemar group is of little importance to mountaineers, its variety of features, the countless scenes which at times are fantastic, and then dizzy and terrifying, and then again pretty and picturesque, all make it of great interest to the excursionist.

Here are two views of the wild, northern bastion of Latemar with the famous lake Carezza. The immagination of shepherds and the Ladin mountainfolk has given rise to the belief that this mysterious world of rocks and the tiny lake placed at its feet are inhabited by wizards, witches and nymphs: according to legend, a rainbow fell into this lake and vanished.

Marmolada

The « Queen of the Dolomites » concludes our tour of the mountains of Gardena and Fassa. The Group of Marmolada occupies a very wide area comprised between the valleys of Cordevole, San Pellegrino and Fassa.

The principal massif rises up almost in the centre of the group, between the Fedaia pass in the North with the large artificial lake — see photograph — and the bare Ombretta valley in he South. This massif is topped by two peaks, standing side by side: Punta Rocca (3,309 m.) and Punta Penia (3,342 m.), which form the highest point in the Dolomites, and crowning them on both sides are Piz Serauta and Gran Vernel. The crest aligning these peaks divides two distinctly different slopes: the northern flank slopes regularly down to Lake Fedaia, with its imposing glacier which recalls the majestic features of the Alpine chain; while in the South stands Marmolada with its sheer face, typical of the Dolomites, which leaps down with a dizzy drop of 800 metres onto the gravel banks of the Ombretta valley.

The first attempt at conquering this spectacular mountain was carried out in 1803, by a group from the Livinallongo valley. It was only in 1860, that the Englishman John Ball managed to climb up to Punta Rocca. However, the honour of being the first to conquer the highest peak of the Pallid Mountains goes to the Viennese Paul Grohmann who, in 1864, reached Marmolada di Penia together with the guides of Ampezzo, Angelo and Fulgenzio Dimai. During the Spring of 1916 and the Autumn of 1917, Marmolada was the stage of bitter fighting between the Austrian and Italian troops, who dug a thick network of tunnels and caverns into the ice in order to escape enemy fire and, in doing so, were under the constant threat of avalanches.

Marmolada, like many other famous summits in the Alps, was conquered with the aid of artificial means created by man. Recently, a very steep cable-way has been constructed, in addition to the chair-lift which runs from Lake Fedaia to Pian dei Fiaconi: it starts from Malga Ciapela and climbs up a gradient of 1,800 m., and in two sections, it reaches all the way up to Forcella Serauta. From here it crosses over a very expressive tract of the glacier and arrives almost to the top of Punta Rocca. Apart from the glacier of Marmolada, which is well provided for by numerous ski-lifts, there are also excellent snow-covered slopes at an altitude of 3,000 m. where you can ski during the summer months from May to October.

Here is a glimpse of the top of Marmolada: extending in the foreground is a strip of the vast glacier slit open by long seracs, while in the background, towering above the others, stands the mighty wall of Sassolungo flanked by Cinque Dita, Sasso Levante and Sassopiatto.
Punta Rocca, with its squat, rocky dome emerging from a sea of ice, can be reached from the topmost station of the cable-way.

The following plate, taken from the summits of Ombretta, shows the mighty wall which constitutes the southern side of Marmolada, furrowed along its entire length by deep chimneys and gullies.

A rope-party among the seracs and bridges of ice of Marmolada: in this dazzling world of ice the silence is broken only by the whistling of the wind and the creaking of the snow under the nailed climbing-boots. Another equally impressive spectacle is the view from the cable-car of the pretty Malga Ciapela basin, which gets smaller and smaller right before your very eyes.

Sunrise from Punta Rocca: above the frothy sea of clouds emerges the peak of Marmolada with its modern cable-car station, as well as the mountains of the Eastern Dolomites, among which you can distinguish Pelmo and Antelao. Below is a very suggestive sun set on Punta Penia with Catinacio in the background. On this page you can admire the awe-inspiring view of the South-West face of Marmolada which hangs over the barren Ombretta pass. This photograph was taken from the San Nicolò pass, a high mountaineering passage separating the valley of the same from the Contrin valley: these two valleys are the ones which penetrate from the Fassa valley into the western sector of the Marmolada group.

The Group of Pale di San Martino

This is the southernmost of the dolomitic groups and also one of the most beautiful and interesting on account of the polychrome variety of its landscape and the splendid architecture of its peaks. This group stands clearly away from the adjacent mountainous complexes, because it is surrounded by wide, deep valleys crossed by frequented roads which make it easily accessible from every direction. In the West, green meadows and woods spread out over Val Cimon, which descends from the Rolle pass down towards the Fiera di Primiero basin; from here a pretty road climbs up to the Cereda pass, southern boundary of the group, and then it enters the middle valley of Cordevole, at Agordo, which marks the north-eastern boundary; finally, in the North we have the Biois valley, which is also a tributary of Cordevole. The structural characteristic of this group lies in the compact base of its dolomitic chains, particularly strong in the western sector; spreading out among these peaks, at an average altitude of 2,600 m., is the Pale plateau, a large limestone table-land occupying the internal lagoon of this ancient coral atoll. The bare undulating plateau, the surrounding vertical walls broken into steep spires and turrets, the mighty bastions decorated with isolated patches of ice, all these go to form a severe and highly suggestive spot: vegetation is very scarce in the heart of this island of cliffs where rock reigns supreme in the dominating majestic dolomitic constructions like Cima Vezzana, the highest point of the group, Cimon della Pala – side plate – and the elegant Pala di San Martino.

The vivid contrast of these bare rocky walls against the thick forests and verdant grasslands which mantle the surrounding valleys, provides one of the most salient panoramic motifs of this region. The extraordinary wealth of the group of Pale is stored in its intact natural surroundings and, for this reason, it has been included together with the state-owned Paneveggio forest and a tract of the solitary Lagorai chain, in the vast natural park of Paneveggio-Pale di San Martino. This park which envelops the upper basin of the Cismon torrent and Travignolo, sums up admirably those elements of the landscape and geological structure as well as the flora and fauna which characterise the dolomitic region. The natural park represents a valid instrument for the preservation of the landscape and the natural biological habitat, and at the same time provides a stimulus to the tourist and induces him into making direct contact with nature: access to those wilder and more expressive areas of the park is facilitated by the State highway which runs through the Rolle pass, and also by the various cable-car and chair-lift services. The choice of excursions is very vast: there are walks through woods and picturesque valleys that clamber over the mountainsides, like Val Venegia and the Canali valley; and also crossings, of a more mountaineering nature, over the Pale chain and the rocky plateau that spreads out at its feet.

In winter there are many opportunities for skiers, thanks to the excellent organisation for tourism and winter sports, on the slopes of Rolle and San Martino di Castrozza, which has acquired its international fame from the fact that it was the site of an ancient pilgrim's rest. The chair-lift of the pass of Rolle-Baita Segantini and the cable-car of Rosetta and Tognola, just to mention a few of the principal services, give access to the fabulous ski-runs and enable you to make some enjoyable skiing excursions in this basin, encircled by the fantastic scenery of the Pale group.

The steep pyramid-shaped Cimon della Pala — at 3,185 m. — towers above the rest and dominates the snow-covered expanses of the Rolle pass, showing off its unmistakable profile that has earned it the merited title of the « Matterhorn of the Dolomites ». Cima della Vezzana — 3,191 m. — stands royally just a step behind, fanning out its rosy face.

92

The picturesque Venegia valley is an oasis of nature lying intact right in the heart of the park of Pale, and enclosed within a steep circle of peaks: between the North face of Cimon della Pala and Cima Vezzana lies the small glacier of Travignolo, which feeds the mountain stream of the same name, while on the left stand the steep faces of Cima dei Bureloni and Cima Val Grande.

Here are some more views of the Rolle pass – 1,989 m. – linked by a very convenient road to the San Martino di Castrozza basin. From this pass, a very popular locality among tourists and winter sports enthusiasts, you can take beautiful walks along the banks at the foot of the Pale mountain chain, in the direction of Val Venegia, passing by the very hospitable shelters of Capanna Cervino and the famous Baita Segantini. The polyhedric pyramid of Cimon della Pala, culminating in the characteristic pointed Becco, is the dominating feature of the landscape: the first ascent on this steep and elegant peak was carried out in 1870, by the Englishman Whitwell, accompanied by the guides Christian Lauener and Santo Siorpaes.

Extending over the southern sector of the Pale group, which is dominated by the majestic Pala di San Martino – 2,987 m., are the sister valleys of Canali and Pradidali that spread out with their bright scenery interlaced with flower - covered meadows and thick fir-woods. In the gravelly basin at the head of the Pradidali valley, where there is also the shelter of the same name, lies a tiny lake whose waters reflect the massive dolomitic turret of Sass Maor. The Pradidali shelter acts as the starting point for the interesting excursions, of a mountaineering nature, in the Pale chain; we recall the path leading to San Martino di Castrozza which passes by the Ball pass and the Pedrotti shelter at Rosetta, and also, the crossing over Cima della Madonna and Sass Maor by the overhead railway, which we show just a glimpse of here together with Cima Wilma and Cima Canali.

The steep cable - way of Col Verde - Rosetta takes you from San Martino di Castrozza right up to the Rosetta plateau, in the heart of the Pale chain. This easy climb up to Rosetta — 2,743 m. — unveils a truly spectacular panorama that extends beyond the dolomitic region; nearby, stands the mighty Pala di San Martino with its vast face spotted with yellow, reminding one of an altar-piece, and dominating the gravelly valley that rises up to the narrow gully of the Ball pass. The photograph below shows a very suggestive sunset on the Rosetta plateau.

The Civetta Group

The isolated and compact Civetta group rises up between the valley of Zoldo and the middle valley of Cordevole, whose main centre is Agordo. The group's structure is quite simple and on the map it is shapped like a huge trident: in fact it consists of a central cluster uniting the higher peaks – Civetta and Piccola Civetta, 3,128 m. and 3,207 m. respectively – and four ramifications which are joined to the central cluster. The North branch comprises a series of huge turrets separated by deep saddles, namely – see photograph below – Torre Coldai, Torre d'Alleghe, Torre Valgrande and finally, linked by a slender crest, Castello di Valgrande and Torre da Lago. The other three ramifications branch out towards the southern side and are represented by the intricate mass of Cantoni di Pelsa, the mighty ridge of Cantoni della Busazza and Civetta Bassa, culminating in Punta di Tomé – 3,004 m.

The numerous shelters and bivouacs scattered all over the Civetta group show the importance given it by mountaineers: at the extreme end of the North branch lies the Sonino al Coldai shelter, the first one constructed in this group, while in the southern sector, you will find the Vazzola shelter lying between Cantoni di Pelsa and Cantoni Busazza; finally, a mention of the tiny Torrani shelter standing at an altitude of 2,984 m. on the eastern flank of the central cluster. The first person to venture up to the highest peak of the group was a chamois-hunter named Simeone De Silvestro, later called Piovanel, after 1855. The first ascent was carried out in 1867 by the Englishman Tuckett. However, even after the easiest way up was discovered, the difficult problem of scaling the North face still remained unsolved: it is an enormous sheer wall, which on account of its steepness is defined the « face of all faces » – the following plate shows a suggestive sunset – towering more than a thousand metres above the gravel pits of the Civetta valley. This wall was affronted and conquered for the first time, in 1895, by Phillmore and Raynor, who traced the so-called «route of the English ». Following this, other less tortuous and more demanding routes were discovered on this spectacular face. Then, in 1925, the « speediest » route to the top was traced by the Bavarian guide, Emil Solleder and Gustav Lettenbauer. Still to this day, as in the past, mountaineers all over the world are attracted by the towers and walls which make the Civetta group the « kingdom of the 6th degree ».

THE DOLOMITES OF BRENTA

Here we are at the conclusion of this fascinating journey across the Dolomites. The group of Brenta, lying West of Trento and the wide Adige basin, in the vicinity of glaciers and the superb peak of Adamello-Presanella and Ortles, stands outside the geographical boundaries of the Dolomites, however, it has some important features in common, namely its geological constitution, the characteristics of its landscape and, its peaks. Furthermore, some of the characteristics which distinguish the Pallid Mountains from the other Alpine chains, such as the prevailing vertical contours, the square-cut profiles, the mighty rocky masses broken into turrets and spires, result as being particularly evident in the Brenta group. As regards its structure, the group consists of a long chain that extends for almost 40 kilometres in the North-East South-West direction, from the point where the Noce torrent widens into the artificial lake of Santa Giustina at the straits of the Sarca river near Stenico. Both the central sector, comprised between Bocca di Tuckett and Bocca di Brenta, as well as the Cima Tosa sector lying South of the latter, represent the most interesting and frequented parts of this hard world of rocks and light, studded here and there with small glaciers: rising up in this region are some of the steepest and towering peaks, imposing masses of Dolomia Principale such as Cima Brenta (3,150 m.) and Torre di Brenta, the characteristic Crozzon di Brenta and Cima Tosa (3,173 m.), which is the highest point in the group. When viewed from the West, the Brenta chain shows a truly massive and severe structure with the outstanding massif of Cima Brenta and Crozzon di Brenta; while on the opposite side, its features become moer rugged in the dominant forms of sharp, steep towers, spires and pinnacles.

Both the Brenta group, as well as Adamello-Presinella, constitute the vastest territory destined to the natural park of Trentino. The dominating feature of the landscape is portrayed by the steep dolomitic architecture of Brenta and, in front, by the vast glaciers and majestic granite peaks of the Adamello-Presinella group, with the wild valley of Genova lying deeply wedged in among them. The group of Brenta also contributes towards this park's wealth in landscape and nature, with its numerous and suggestive valleys hollowed out and radiating from the central massif; standing out among these are Vallesinella with its picturesque waterfalls, Val Brenta, the delightful Val d'Agola and the Tovel valley, which guards the famous lake whose waters periodically assume a characteristic red colour due to the presence of an unicellular alga, creating an exceptionally rare phenomenon.

There are various valleys with spectacular ranges of scenery, which contribute towards completely isolating this dolomitic oasis: here is the Rendena valley which bands the western flank of Brenta with its thick, dark fir-tres, followed by the mountainous Meledrio valley that descends from the Campo Carlo Magno pass down towards the valley of the Sun; and here, on the eastern side, we have the wide open Non valley with its castles and gently sloping terraces of fruit orchards, and the bright plateau of Andalo and Molveno with the lake of the same name. Among the main tourist centres scattered around the Brenta group, there is Molveno which offers easy access to the eastern side, with the aid of chair-lifts that climb up towards Croz dell'Altissimo and Madonna di Campiglio, lying at the head of the Rendena valley in a beautiful basin rich in woods and meadows, pretty little lakes and bubbly mountain streams. Today, Madonna di Campiglio is a well-known international holiday resort and winter sports station and, the most renowned in the Alpine range, thanks to the excellent organisation for tourism and the modern lift services, among which is the cable-way system linking Pradalago, Folgarida, Spinale and Grosté.

After this brief introduction, we now continue deep into the heart of the group: following the trails which link the numerous shelters and, in particular, the aerial « Via delle Bocchette » which climbs at a very high altitude along ridges, small glaciers and sheer faces and enables us to admire, from close up, the wild and spectacular world of the Brenta Dolomites.

A delightful walk along a path through the woods, cheered up by the dense patches of Rhododendrons, will lead you from Madonna di Campiglio up to Lake Nambino, situated at the foot of mount Pancugolo. On the other side of the Madonna di Campiglio basin tower the snow-covered majestic peaks of the central sector of the Brenta group, with Cima Brenta dominating over the others.

The beautiful
Campiglio
basin opens
up in the splendid
framework
of mountains
and woods:
Madonna
di Campiglio,
an elegant
and bustling
holiday resort,
is a famous
winter sports
station and the
principal
departure
point for summer
excursions in
the group
of Brenta.

106

The festive flowering of Rhododendrons creates a lively contrast against the severe dolomitic masses still covered with snow: here we are right on the part which separates Vallesinella from the Brenta Alta valley, with the dominating massif of Cima Tosa and the unmistakable Crozzon di Brenta towering up above.

Picturesque Vallesinella, which is cut off from the Madonna di Campiglio basin by mount Spinale, is one of the most popular destinations of excursionists and, is also one of the main entrances to the central sector of the group of Brenta. On this page is a view of this solitary valley, as seen from the road which runs along the initial tract, clothed by the cheery and warm autumnal colours of the beeches and larches. The imposing Cima Brenta and Cima Quintino Sella rise up in the background, and among these peaks opens up Bocca di Tuckett. Vallesinella has very rich vegetation and numerous frothy waterfalls, formed by a branch of the Sarca river – see plate on the right showing the Vallesinella di Sopra waterfall – and this is why it is regarded as one of the most beautiful spots in the natural park of Adamello-Brenta.

Via delle Bocchette

The dolomitic mountains, composed of numerous long ledges, chimneys and saddles, are ideal for establishing those « ready-equipped mountaineering routes » and the « rock-piton ladder routes » which offer an attractive invitation to draw near to this world high up in the mountains: in fact, stable fittings have been installed along these routes, such as narrow bridges, ropes and metallic ladders fixed to the rocks, which allow even non-experienced climbers to cross over certain passages that normally prove extremely difficult. The Company of Tridentini Mountaineers has established a truly vast complex of rock-piton ladder routes across the Brenta Dolomites forming the « Via delle Bocchette » (which means passages through the gaps in the mountains). This spectacular itinerary links the northern and southern sectors of the Brenta group via this series of passages across the gaps between the peaks in the central chain.

The Via delle Bocchette was constructed during the course of many years, and was gradually extended by the numerous tracts running from the Tosa sector up to the Grosté pass, and leading North of the latter, on the flank of Pietra Grande, thus taking in all the principal shelters; besides this it is also linked to other trails in the group, such as the panoramic Osvaldo Orsi trail and that of Brentei. This network of trails is so vast and articulated that it is possible to make an infinity of excursions, each different and varied in character. On the following pages you will find our description of the main tracts of the Via delle Bocchette, and at the same time you will have the opportunity of admiring ,from close up, the most famous peaks and spectacular sights of the Dolomites of Brenta.

The Maria e Alberto shelter of Brentei – 2,120 m. – stands in an exceptionally panoramic position, at the point where the Brentei valley merges with the upper Brenta valley: rising up on one side, are the tortured faces of Punte di Campiglio and Cima Mandron – on the left – and opposite them, towards the South, stands the mighty Crozzon di Brenta – 3,135 m. – jutting out from the gigantic massif of Cima Tosa; the chief ascents on Crozzon, one of the group's most difficult peaks with its steep walls and pointed North corner, were carried out in about 1882, by the guide Matteo Nicolussi and others. The Brentei shelter, which can be reached via the Brenta valley, is an important starting point for excursions in the central sector of Brenta.

If you climb from the Brentei shelter up the valley of the same name you will arrive at the Via delle Bocchette on the SOSAT trail, which terminates at the small Alimonta shelter situated on the magnificent, rocky balcony of Pian dei Armi at the foot of Torre della Brenta.. Even the most recent tract of this interesting itinerary, which begins at Bocca di Tuckett and crosses Spallone di Massodi, is joined to this part of Via delle Bocchette. For the moment, we shall continue towards Bocca di Brenta in order to enter the most famous and spectacular part: the trail unwinds along the eastern walls of Torre di Brenta, Sfulmini and Campanile Alto, making use of the overhead ledges suspended at dizzy heights over the gravel banks of Busa degli Sfulmini. We are confronted by the majestic view of Campanile Basso, standing tall and elegant before us. After Campanile Basso, the trail winds around the base of Brenta Alta, and then, finally, joins Bocca di Brenta, from where it descends to the Tosa shelter. The scene on this page shows a tract of the Bartolomeo Figari path leading along the ridge which cuts horizontally through Torre di Brenta.

Here we have the superb monolith of Campanile Basso – 2,877 m. – which can be seen from the Arturo Castelli path. Campanile Basso, which rises up isolated between Cima Brenta Alta and Campanile Alto, was conquered for the first time in 1899, by the Austrians Ampferer and Berger. Preceding this was the unsuccessful attempt made by Carlo Garbari who reached up to the terrace that now bears his name.

This fantastic tower can be viewed also in the photograph below, taken from a rock-piton ladder route on the Otto Gottstein trail, which terminates at the Bocca di Brenta above the Pedrotti shelter at Tosa.

The next plate was taken from Busa degli Sfulmini on the Osvaldo Orsi trail, that links the Tosa shelter via Bocca di Tuckett. This trail unwinds at the foot of the East side of the central chain, hundreds of metres below the ➤➤ Via delle Bocchette: we can this way admire a tract of the itinerary, previously described, which is dominated by the powerful mass of Brenta Alta – 2,960 m. – and the tall, slender Campanile Basso.

We are still on the Osvaldo Orsi trail, just before crossing over Bocca di Tuckett, which is dominated by the beautiful face of Cima Quintino Sella, named after the founder of the Italian Mountaineering Club. The Tuckett shelter can be seen in the photograph below, situated at the foot of the rocky tower of Castelletto Inferiore.

On the right, you can glimpse the distinct incision of Bocca di Tuckett, at the foot of Cima Sella, with the tongue of ice that forms Vedretta di Tuckett descending from it.

Another tract of Via delle Bocchette, opened only a few years ago, begins from Bocca di Tuckett, and unveils truly spectacular sights of the scenery of the Brenta Dolomites. Here is a passage of the Foresti Pedrotti trail, following the ledge which crosses Cima Brenta: down below, at the bottom of the valley, you can just glimpse the tiny blue patch of Lake Molveno. The « Scala degli Amici » (meaning ladder of friends) enables you to climb up to an altitude of 3,000 metres, on top of Spallone dei Massodi which is the highest point in the whole Via delle Bocchette; emerging in front of us are Cima Molveno and Cima dei Armi.

From the massive shoulder of Massodi, along the Oliva de Tassis Route, you descend towards Vedretta dei Brentei; the views of the yellow walls of Crozzon di Brenta and the Cima Tosa massif accompany this tract of the path. With the aid of a long series of iron steps you can climb over this last barrier of rock which overhangs Vedretta dei Brentei.

Now we have arrived at the final part of Via delle Bocchette, which is Via Brentari linking the Tosa and Silvio Agostini shelters by passing underneath the southern bastion of Cima Tosa. Often, if you leave the shelter at sunrise, you can view the fantastic sight of the dark peaks of Cima dei Lasteri and Croz dell'Altissimo emerging from a sea of frothy clouds. Via Brentari is also the starting point of the easy climb up to Cima Margherita, which unveils an extremely vast panorama: in the foreground is the western face of Brenta Alta and also Campanile Basso.

This stretch of Via Brentari is dominated by the grand amphitheatre formed out of the southern wall of Cima Tosa. From the Tosa massif rises the highest peak of the group – 3,173 m. – which was reached for the first time, in 1865, by the rope-party led by Giuseppe Loss of Primiero.

You leave the Via delle Bocchette to climb up the Tosa peak: a brief rest on the spacious ledge before tackling the final climb to the top.

Continuing on Via Brentari you reach Sella della Tosa, 2,860 m.; the view is magnificent from the central chain of the group, with Campanile Alto and Brenta Alta, and Campanile Basso rising up between them.

The next plate depicts autumn in the Brenta group. The vast forests are splashed with the red and yellow hues of the larches, re-echoing the golden light of the sunset on the beautiful Dolomite peaks.

Here is an impressive view of Bocca della Tosa. Climbing down along Vedretta d'Ambies, between the summit of the same and Castei della Tosa, you will arrive at the Silvio Agostini shelter, 2,410 metres. This tiny shelter is encircled by a pointed series of peaks called Castei, ending in Punta L'Ideale and the awe-inspiring East face of Cima d'Ambies. You can then go from the Agostini shelter to the Fratelli Garberi shelter — 2,489 m. — either by following the Ettore Castiglioni trail, or by taking the Ideale trail from Bocca della Tosa.

Here we are at the Fratelli Garberi shelter at Dodici Apostoli, situated on an extremely panoramic terrace, at the boundary line of Vedretta di Pratofiorito. At the foot of Cima Dodici Apostoli, a chapel has been dug out of the rock, facing the valley with its huge cross, which is dedicated to the fallen soldiers. A final mention of the Gustavo Vidi trail, which runs from Passo del Grosté to the Graffer shelter, situated on the Pietra Grande massif. The latter is the highest peak in the northern chain of the Dolomites of Brenta.

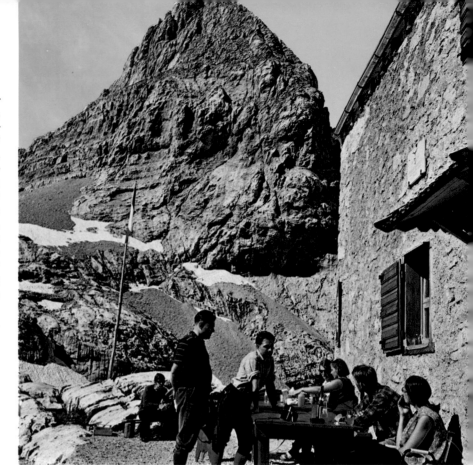

© Copyright by Plurigraf Narni - Terni
Tutti i diritti riservati
Riproduzione anche parziale vietata
Stampato in Italia dalla Plurigraf 1985 Narni - Terni
Fotolito: S.A.R. Offset - via di Pietralata 198 - tel. 4500345 - Roma